olive

101 QUICK FIX DISHES

D0582508

1 3 5 7 9 10 8 6 4 2

Published in 2007 by BBC Books,
an imprint of Ebury Publishing
A Random House Group Company

Copyright © Woodlands Books 2007

All photographs © **olive** magazine
All the recipes contained in this book first appeared in **olive** magazine

The Random House Group Limited Reg. No. 954009

Addresses for companies within the Random House Group can be found at
www.randomhouse.co.uk

A CIP catalogue record for this book is available from the British Library

The Random House Group Limited makes every effort to ensure that the
papers used in our books are made from trees that have been legally
sourced from well-managed and credibly certified forests. Our paper
procurement policy can be found on www.randomhouse.co.uk

Printed and bound by Firmengruppe APPL, aprinta druck, Wemding, Germany

ISBN: 9780563539025

olive

101 QUICK FIX DISHES
no-fuss food in an instant

Editor
Janine Ratcliffe

BBC
BOOKS

Contents

Introduction 6

Introduction

At **olive** we believe you don't have to spend all day in the kitchen to create gorgeous food. Whether you want an after-work supper, a casual lunch for friends or a comforting TV-dinner for one, we know simple, fresh meals can be on the table in half an hour or less.

With an emphasis on easy-to-find ingredients and uncomplicated methods, these imaginative recipes are guaranteed to wow your friends without making a serious dent in your time. We've also included dishes that can be put together after a quick trip to the shops on the way home, to save you more precious time.

In *101 Quick Fix Dishes* you'll find dishes to suit every season and mood: whether you're after a fresh summer salad, a spicy stir-fry or an easy pudding. Each recipe has been carefully selected by the **olive** team for their speed and achievability, and you will want to make recipes like *Dead good spaghetti carbonara* pictured opposite (see page 80 for the recipe), again and again.

As always, all the recipes have been thoroughly tested in the **olive** kitchen to make sure they taste fabulous and work for you first time.

Janine Ratcliffe

Janine Ratcliffe
olive magazine

Notes and Conversions

NOTES ON THE RECIPES

• Where possible, we use humanely reared meats, free-range chickens and eggs, and unrefined sugar.

• Eggs are large unless stated otherwise. Pregnant women, elderly people, babies and toddlers, and anyone who is unwell should avoid eating raw and partially cooked eggs.

APPROXIMATE WEIGHT CONVERSIONS

• All the recipes in this book are listed with metric measurements.

• Cup measurements, which are used by cooks in Australia and America, have not been listed here as they vary from ingredient to ingredient. Please use kitchen scales to measure dry/solid ingredients.

OVEN TEMPERATURES

gas	°C	fan °C	°F	description
¼	110	90	225	Very cool
½	120	100	250	Very cool
1	140	120	275	Cool or slow
2	150	130	300	Cool or slow
3	160	140	325	Warm
4	180	160	350	Moderate
5	190	170	375	Moderately hot
6	200	180	400	Fairly hot
7	220	200	425	Hot
8	230	210	450	Very hot
9	240	220	475	Very hot

SPOON MEASURES

· Spoon measurements are level unless otherwise specified.

· 1 teaspoon (tsp) = 5ml

· 1 tablespoon (tbsp) = 15ml

· 1 Australian tablespoon = 20ml (cooks in Australia should measure 3 teaspoons where 1 tablespoon is specified in a recipe)

APPROXIMATE LIQUID CONVERSIONS

metric	imperial	US
60ml	2fl oz	¼ cup
125ml	4fl oz	½ cup
175ml	6fl oz	¾ cup
225ml	8fl oz	1 cup
300ml	10fl oz/½ pint	1¼ cups
450ml	16fl oz	2 cups/1 pint
600ml	20fl oz/1 pint	2½ cups
1 litre	35fl oz/1¾ pints	1 quart

Please note that an Australian cup is 250ml, ¾ cup is 190ml, ½ cup is 125ml, ¼ cup is 60ml.

Smoked mackerel pâté

15 minutes

smoked mackerel 300g, skin and any
   bones removed
unsalted butter 75g, very soft
crème fraîche 150g
hot horseradish sauce 1 tbsp
lemon 1, grated zest
caraway seeds 1 tbsp, lightly toasted
   (optional)
rye bread 4 slices, toasted, to serve

■ Put the smoked mackerel and butter
in a food processor with plenty of black
pepper and whiz until the butter has
blended with the fish. Stir in the
remaining ingredients, except the bread,
and pile into a dish. Serve with hot
toasted rye bread. **Serves 6**

Try using hot smoked salmon or trout
instead of mackerel for a variation.

Seared sesame tuna

20 minutes

soy sauce 2 tbsp
runny honey 1 tbsp
tuna steaks 2, very lean, thick-cut
sesame seeds 2 tbsp, toasted
spring onions 4, shredded lengthways
coriander leaves a handful
cucumber, ¼ seeded and cut into strips

DIPPING SAUCE
soy sauce 2 tbsp
sesame oil 1 tsp
lime 1, juiced
red chilli 1, finely chopped

■ Mix together the soy sauce and runny honey to make a marinade. Marinate the tuna steaks for 10 minutes.

■ Sear the tuna in a hot pan for 20 seconds each side, then roll in sesame seeds and leave for 5 minutes.

■ Mix the spring onions, coriander and cucumber. Slice the steaks into strips. Mix the dipping sauce ingredients together and serve in a dish alongside the tuna and a pile of salad. **Serves 2**

Make sure your tuna is fresh for this as you'll be eating it very rare.

Green pea and tarragon soup

20 minutes

onion 1 large, chopped

butter for frying

potato 1 medium, peeled and diced

vegetable or chicken stock fresh, cube or
   concentrate, made up to 1 litre

frozen petit pois 400g

tarragon leaves chopped to make 2 tbsp

■ Fry the onion in a knob of butter until tender, add the potato and stock and simmer until the potato is very soft. Add the peas and tarragon, simmer for 3 minutes then blend to a smooth soup. Season and serve. **Serves 4**

Petit pois are picked earlier than standard peas and have a much sweeter flavour.

Hot and sour cucumber salad

15 minutes

cucumber 1, peeled
cherry tomatoes 250g
shallots 2, finely sliced
bird's eye chillies 2, split open
rice wine vinegar or cider vinegar 1 tbsp
coriander leaves a handful

■ Finely slice the cucumber and halve the cherry tomatoes. Toss these with the shallots and chillies, season and dress with vinegar. Scatter coriander over.
Serves 6

Bird's eye chillies are extremely hot so just split and toss through the salad to add heat, rather than chopping, and don't be tempted to bite into one.

Pink grapefruit salad

30 minutes

pink grapefruit 4

oil for frying

shallots 3, finely sliced

palm sugar or soft brown sugar ½ tsp

mint leaves a large handful

cashew nuts 50g, toasted and roughly
    chopped

coriander leaves a large handful

■ Cut the pith off the grapefruit with a sharp knife, then cut out the segments and put them in a bowl. Heat a little oil in a small frying pan and fry the shallots until browned, add the sugar and stir until it dissolves. Leave to cool.

■ Spread the grapefruit segments out on a serving plate and scatter over the shallot mixture, mint leaves, cashews and coriander. **Serves 6**

You want to get the shallots nicely crisp and golden to add extra texture to this salad.

Smoked salmon on rye with caper soured cream

15 minutes

soured cream 142ml carton
capers 1 tbsp, rinsed and sliced
rye bread 8 slices
gherkins 2 large, roughly chopped
smoked salmon or **gravadlax** 100g
mixed salad leaves 1 bag, dressed with
   vinaigrette
lemon 1, cut into wedges

■ Mix the soured cream and capers together and season. Spoon the mixture on top of the rye bread. Scatter the gherkins over the soured cream mixture and arrange the smoked salmon or gravadlax on top. Sprinkle black pepper over and serve with the dressed salad and a lemon wedge. **Serves 4**

Mix a tablespoon of Dijon mustard into the soured cream to give this an extra bit of kick.

Chickpea and pomegranate dip with pitta crisps

30 minutes

pitta breads 6–8

extra-virgin olive oil 100ml, plus extra
  for the crisps

chickpeas 2 × 400g tins, drained

lemon 1, juiced

red chillies 2, seeded and chopped

garlic 1 clove, finely chopped

cumin seeds 2 tsp, toasted in a dry
  frying pan

red onion 1 small, finely chopped

mint or **parsley leaves** a small bunch,
  finely chopped

pomegranate molasses or **tamarind
  paste** thinned down with
  2 tbsp water

■ Heat the oven to 200C/fan 180C/gas 6.
Cut the pittas into triangles and separate
the layers. Brush with olive oil, season
and bake for 7–8 minutes until crisp
and golden.

■ Put the chickpeas, 100ml olive oil,
lemon juice, chillies and garlic in a food
processor, season and pulse until just
crushed. Remove and mix in the cumin
seeds, red onion and mint or parsley.
Season. Drizzle with pomegranate
molasses and serve with warm pitta
crisps. **Serves 8**

You can buy pomegranate
molasses, a sweet and sour syrup,
at some supermarkets or a Middle
Eastern grocer.

Whole baked brie with honey and pecans

20 minutes

brie 1 small whole, about 300g

olive oil

thyme 2 sprigs, leaves stripped

pecans a handful, halved and toasted

runny honey 2 tbsp

crusty bread to serve

■ Heat the oven to 200C/fan 180C/gas 6. Put the brie in an ovenproof dish, make a few cuts in the top, drizzle with olive oil and sprinkle the thyme over. Cover with foil and bake for 5–10 minutes until gooey. Sprinkle with pecans, drizzle with honey and serve with warm crusty bread.

Serves 4

Serve this brie with whole cooked baby new potatoes for dipping.

Bacon, egg and spinach salad

20 minutes

ciabatta loaf ¼, cut into chunks
olive oil 3 tbsp + a little extra
red wine vinegar 1 tbsp
wholegrain mustard 1 tsp
eggs 2
streaky bacon 6 rashers
young spinach 2 handfuls, washed

■ To make the croutons, toss the ciabatta chunks in olive oil then bake until golden.

■ Whisk together the olive oil, the red wine vinegar and the wholegrain mustard to make the dressing.

■ Fry or poach the eggs in barely simmering water for 5 minutes. Grill the bacon until crisp and break into pieces. Toss the spinach and bacon with a little of the dressing. Divide between 2 plates, top with the croutons and an egg. Drizzle with the remaining dressing. **Serves 2**

For a more delicate salad, top with boiled and halved quail's eggs.

Soft boiled egg and chorizo salad

15 minutes

eggs 4
olive oil 3 tbsp
wholegrain mustard 1 tbsp
lemon ½, juiced
chorizo 100g, cut into chunks or sliced
ciabatta ½ a loaf, made into chunky
    croutons (see previous recipe)
rocket 100g

■ Put the eggs in a pan of boiling water and cook for 4 minutes, then cool under running water for a minute.

■ Whisk the olive oil, mustard and lemon juice together. Season. Arrange the chorizo, croutons and rocket leaves on 4 serving plates. Shell the eggs, then roughly break them in half and add to the chorizo and rocket. Drizzle the dressing over and serve. **Serves 4**

This salad would work well with other peppery leaves, such as watercress.

Spinach, bacon and new potato salad

20 minutes

small new potatoes 250g
streaky bacon 6 rashers
young spinach 2 handfuls
parmesan shavings a handful

DRESSING
olive oil 3 tbsp
red wine vinegar 1 tbsp
wholegrain mustard 1 tbsp

■ Whisk together all of the dressing ingredients.
■ Boil the potatoes until tender, about 10 minutes. Grill the bacon until crisp and golden, then cool and break into pieces. Toss the spinach and potatoes with half the dressing. Divide between 2 plates and top with the bacon. Drizzle with extra dressing and scatter the parmesan shavings over. **Serves 2**

Try frying the potatoes in a little olive oil after boiling for a crunchy texture.

Bocconcini, prosciutto and herb salad

15 minutes

herb salad 1 bag, about 100g

tomatoes 2 large, cut into wedges

avocado 1, peeled and sliced

bocconcini 10, halved

prosciutto 4 slices

pine nuts 2 tbsp, toasted

olive oil

lemon 1, juiced

■ Tip the salad leaves into a large shallow bowl. Add the tomatoes, avocado and bocconcini. Grill or dry fry the prosciutto slices until they crisp up and then break them into pieces over the salad. Scatter over the pine nuts. Dress with olive oil, lemon juice and lots of seasoning. Serve with crusty bread. **Serves 2**

Bocconcini are baby mozzarella – use a regular ball, torn into pieces, if you can't find them.

Warm brie, chicory and bacon salad

15 minutes

cider vinegar 1 tbsp
olive oil 3 tbsp
chicory 2 heads, leaves separated
streaky bacon 6 rashers, grilled until crisp
   then broken into pieces
brie 100g, sliced
chives a small bunch, snipped

■ Whisk the cider vinegar and olive oil together to make the dressing. Toss the chicory and bacon with the dressing and arrange on 2 heatproof plates. Top with slices of brie then grill until melted, sprinkle with chives and serve. **Serves 2**

Chill the brie in the fridge for 30 minutes first to make it easier to slice.

Asparagus, walnut and goat's cheese salad

15 minutes

asparagus 4 bunches, trimmed
sherry vinegar 2 tbsp
walnut oil 4 tbsp
red chicory 2 heads, separated or
   2 handfuls **salad leaves**
yellow or **red cherry tomatoes** 300g,
   halved
walnuts 100g, toasted and roughly
   chopped
goat's cheese 100g, crumbled
chives a small bunch, snipped into short
   lengths

■ Blanch the asparagus in boiling salted water for 1 minute, drain and cool in iced water, then drain again. In a small bowl, mix the vinegar with the walnut oil. Season. Layer the asparagus, chicory, tomatoes and walnuts on a large platter. Pour the dressing over and then scatter with goat's cheese and chives. **Serves 4**

Use quite a firm goat's cheese for this – it'll be easier to crumble.

Bloody Mary shots with avocado toasts

30 minutes

avocado 1
red onion ½, very finely sliced
tomato 1, diced
lemon ½, juiced
long skinny baguette 8 thin slices,
    toasted

BLOODY MARY MIX
tomato juice 500ml
celery salt ¼ tsp (find it by the spices)
horseradish sauce 1 tsp
vodka 4 tbsp
Tabasco a dash
Worcestershire sauce a dash
lemon ½, juiced

■ Mix together all the Bloody Mary ingredients and season, adding Tabasco, Worcestershire sauce and lemon juice to taste. Chill.

■ Peel and finely dice the avocado, mix with the red onion and tomato and a squeeze of lemon juice and season well. Pile the avocado mixture on to the baguette toasts.

■ Serve a shot glass of Bloody Mary (give it a quick stir before you serve it) with two toasts on the side. **Serves 4**

Try using a flavoured vodka such as pepper or lemon to bump up the flavours in the Bloody Mary.

Prawn salad with grapefruit vinaigrette

20 minutes

grapefruit 1

watercress 100g, any big woody stalks removed

cooked, peeled king prawns 150g

avocado 1, peeled and sliced

olive oil 2 tbsp

wholegrain mustard 1 tsp

■ Using a sharp knife, peel the grapefruit then segment. Do this over a bowl to catch the juice. Squeeze what's left of the grapefruit to collect the rest of the juice.

■ Divide the watercress, prawns and avocado between 2 plates. Scatter the grapefruit segments over. Whisk the olive oil and mustard with 3 tbsp of the grapefruit juice. Drizzle over the salad and serve. **Serves 2**

Try pink or red grapefruit for this. They will look pretty and have a sweeter flavour than normal grapefruit.

Thai beef noodle salad

15 minutes

medium rice noodles 125g (Blue Dragon are good)
sirloin steak 1, about 300g, trimmed of fat
cucumber 1 small, cut into ribbons
red chilli 1, shredded
coriander leaves a small handful

DRESSING
Thai sweet chilli sauce 3 tbsp
lime 1, juiced
fish sauce 1 tbsp

■ Put the noodles in a large bowl and pour boiling water over. Leave until tender then drain and rinse well with cold water.

■ Heat a griddle (chargrill) or heavy frying pan until very hot. Oil and season the steak then cook for 1–2 minutes each side, depending on how thick it is. Rest for 5 minutes.

■ Stir together the dressing ingredients. Slice the steak. Toss the noodles, cucumber and chilli with the steak and dressing. Scatter coriander over and serve.
Serves 2

To cut ribbons from a cucumber, peel along the length with a potato peeler, turning the cucumber as you go.

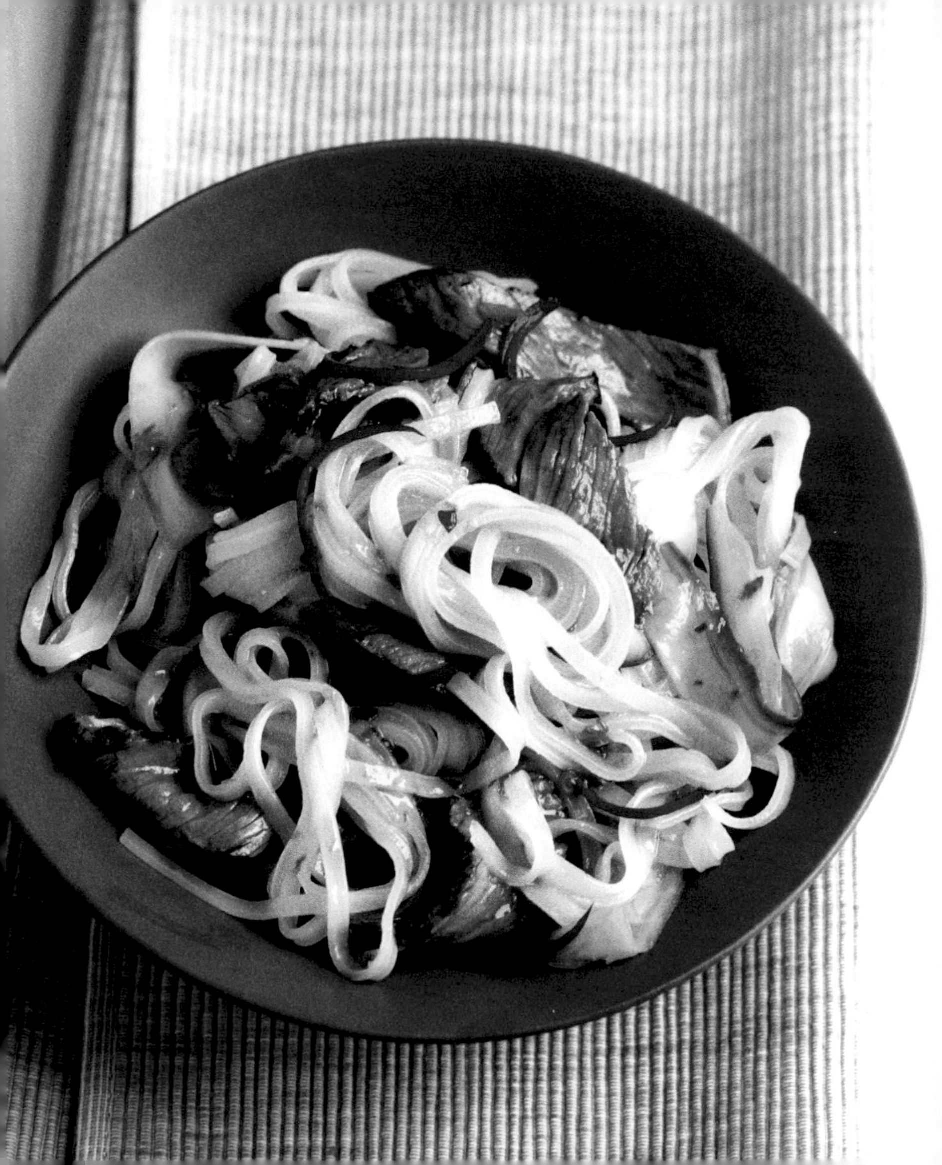

Beef carpaccio

20 minutes

beef fillet 250g (you'll need a nice thick
     piece of centre cut)
rocket leaves a handful
parmesan or Grana Padano shaved with
     a potato peeler

DRESSING
egg yolks 2
olive oil 100ml
lemon 1, juiced
English mustard ½ tsp

■ To make the dressing, put the egg yolks
in a blender or mini processor (or use a
hand whisk) and add the olive oil in a
steady stream. Season with lemon juice,
mustard, salt and pepper and mix well.
■ Using a very sharp, large knife, cut
slices of beef as thinly as you can. Lay
these on a plate and cover them with
clingfilm to stop them colouring. (If you
put a layer of baking parchment or
clingfilm between the layers you'll be
able to separate them out easily later.)
■ To serve, place the beef slices on a
platter or individual plates, heap some
rocket leaves in the middle and drizzle
the dressing around the edge. Finish with
parmesan shavings. **Serves 6**

Put the beef into the freezer for
30 minutes to firm it up and make it
easier to slice very thinly.

Bacon, mozzarella and pine nut salad

15 minutes

salad leaves 2 handfuls
mozzarella 1 ball, torn into pieces
pine nuts 2 tbsp, toasted
thin streaky bacon 8 rashers, grilled until
   crisp then broken into pieces

DRESSING
olive oil 2 tbsp
red wine vinegar 1 tbsp

■ Whisk together the olive oil and vinegar and season. Toss together the salad leaves with the mozzarella, pine nuts and dressing. Divide between 2 plates and scatter the bacon over.
Serves 2

Always toast pine nuts before adding them to salads, as it helps to bring out their flavour.

Roasted garlic and thyme chicken

30 minutes

chicken breasts 4, skin on
garlic 3 cloves, crushed
thyme 3 sprigs, leaves stripped
butter 50g
red onions 2, cut into slim wedges
pancetta cubes 140g
oil for roasting
mixed salad 150g, dressed to serve

■ Heat the oven to 200C/fan 180/gas 6. Put the chicken skin-side-up in a small roasting tin. Mix together the garlic, thyme and butter and dot over the chicken. Scatter around the red onions and pancetta and drizzle with oil. Roast for 20 minutes until the chicken has cooked through and the onions are softened. Divide the salad between 4 plates and top with the red onions, pancetta and chicken. **Serves 4**

Pancetta cubes, also called *cubetti di pancetta*, are sold in packs at most supermarkets. Bacon lardons will also work.

Roast chicken risotto

30 minutes

butter for frying
onion 1, finely chopped
garlic 2 cloves, finely chopped
risotto rice 350g, carnaroli or arborio
white wine 1 large glass
chicken or vegetable stock fresh, cube or
    concentrate, made up to 1.5 litres,
    heated to simmering
frozen peas a large handful, defrosted
cooked chicken about 200g, torn into
    strips, no skin
parmesan 50g, grated

■ Melt a knob of butter in a large pan, add the onion and garlic and cook until soft and translucent. Stir in the rice until coated with butter. Add the wine and stir until evaporated. Add the stock a ladle at a time until the rice is cooked but still with a little bite (add the peas and chicken in the last 5 minutes of cooking to heat through). The rice should be creamy but firm to the bite. Stir in the parmesan. **Serves 4**

For an extra rich risotto, stir in a knob of butter at the end of cooking.

Thai green chicken curry

20 minutes

oil 1 tbsp
skinless chicken breasts 4 small, thinly sliced
green curry paste 1–2 tbsp, depending on how hot you like it
coconut milk 400ml tin
green beans 100g, trimmed
courgette 1 small, halved lengthways and thinly sliced
lime 1, juiced
coriander leaves a handful
rice to serve

■ Heat a large saucepan and add the oil. Cook the chicken for 3 minutes until it starts to brown. Add the curry paste and cook, stirring, for 1 minute until fragrant. Then add the coconut milk, stir and reduce the heat to a gentle simmer. Cook for 10 minutes, then add the beans and courgette. Cook for 3 minutes until the vegetables are just tender. Remove from heat and season to taste with lime juice and stir through the coriander. Serve with boiled rice. **Serves 4**

Look for authentic Thai curry pastes in larger supermarkets or Asian grocers.

Chicken with couscous salad

20 minutes

---

couscous 200g

red pepper 1, cut into chunks

spring onions 4, sliced

raisins 50g

chicken stock fresh, cube or concentrate,
  made up to 300ml

pine nuts 2 tbsp, toasted

lemon 1, juiced

roasted chicken breasts 2, sliced, skin
  discarded

salad leaves 4 handfuls

■ Put the couscous, pepper, spring onions and raisins in a heatproof bowl. Pour the chicken stock over, cover and leave for 10 minutes.

■ Fluff up the couscous with a fork and stir in the pine nuts and lemon juice. Season and serve with the sliced chicken and salad leaves. **Serves 4**

You could use roasted red peppers from a jar for this to add extra sweetness.

Very quick chicken curry

30 minutes

oil for frying
onion 1, chopped
curry paste 2 tbsp, such as Madras
skinless chicken thighs or thigh fillets 4
tomatoes 4, chopped
young spinach 100g
natural yoghurt 4 tbsp
coriander leaves a handful
basmati rice or naan bread to serve

■ Heat a little oil in a deep non-stick frying pan (with a lid) and add the onion. Fry for about 3 minutes until tender then stir in the curry paste and fry for a minute. Add the chicken and tomatoes and a splash of water, cover and cook for 15–20 minutes until just cooked through. Fold in the spinach until it just wilts then stir in the yoghurt and coriander. Season. Serve with rice or naan bread. **Serves 2**

Madras paste has quite a bit of heat to it – choose a milder one if you like.

Butterflied chicken with pesto cream

<u>20 minutes</u>

chicken breasts 2 skinless, butterflied
olive oil
pesto 2 tbsp
half-fat crème fraîche 3 tbsp
watercress and **cherry tomatoes** to serve

■ Heat a griddle (chargrill) pan. Brush the chicken with a little olive oil and season well. Cook on both sides for 2–3 minutes until grill-marked and cooked through. Mix together the pesto and crème fraîche. Serve the chicken with the watercress, cherry tomatoes and the pesto cream. **Serves 2**

To butterfly chicken breasts, slice in half horizontally (but not all the way through) then open them out like a book and gently roll to flatten.

Rice noodles with sticky lime and chilli chicken

20 minutes

chicken thigh fillets 4, skin on

lime 1, juiced

sweet chilli sauce 1 tbsp, plus extra
to serve

rice noodles 125g, soaked following
packet instructions

coriander leaves a small bunch, chopped

mint leaves a small bunch, finely chopped

cucumber ½ peeled into ribbons with
a potato peeler

■ Mix the chicken in a bowl with half the lime juice, and the sweet chilli sauce. Season. Put on a baking sheet, flattened out as much as possible, and grill on each side for about 4 minutes or until cooked through. Make sure you finish on the skin side so it crisps up.

■ Drain the noodles and stir through the rest of the lime juice, the herbs and cucumber. Season well. Serve the noodles with the chicken on top and a little bowl of chilli sauce on the side. **Serves 2**

Remove the chicken skin before marinating for a lower fat version of this dish.

Chicken with walnuts and soured cream

15 minutes

cooked chicken breast 200g, cut
   into strips
walnuts 50g, chopped
cherry tomatoes 4, quartered
spring onion 1, chopped
olive oil 2 tbsp
white wine vinegar 1 tsp
Dijon mustard 1 tsp
soured cream 2 tbsp
mint leaves small handful, chopped

■ Put the chicken, walnuts, tomatoes and spring onion into a bowl and mix lightly.
■ Make the dressing by whisking the olive oil with the vinegar, then whisking in the mustard and soured cream. Fold the salad and dressing together and scatter thickly with the mint. **Serves 2**

Always chop soft herbs such as mint and basil at the last moment to stop them discolouring.

Five-spice roast duck breast

<u>30 minutes</u>

duck breasts 4, look for free-range
Chinese five-spice 1 tsp
olive oil for frying
star anise 2, broken in half
pak choi 4, halved
spring onions 4, cut into lengths
soy sauce 2 tbsp
chicken stock fresh, cube or concentrate,
    made up to 100ml
runny honey 2 tsp

Using just the duck breast rather than a whole bird makes it easier to control the cooking to get perfectly tender meat.

■ Cut slashes through the skin and fat of each duck breast, making sure you don't cut into the flesh. Rub the duck breasts with the five-spice and season well. Heat a little oil in a heavy frying pan and when it is really hot add the duck breasts, skin-side down. Turn the heat down a little and fry for 8–10 minutes or until the skin is very crisp and brown and the fat has started to melt out from under it. Tip out any excess fat.

■ Turn the breasts over and add the star anise to the pan. Cook for another 5 minutes or until the duck breasts feel firm to the touch but not too solid – you want them pink in the middle. Take the duck out and leave to rest for 5 minutes.

■ Meanwhile, add the pak choi to the pan with the spring onions and cook briefly. Add the rest of the ingredients and bubble together briefly. Plate the duck, pak choi and spring onions and spoon the sauce over. **Serves 4**

Chicken quesadillas

20 minutes

flour tortillas 4
cooked chicken breast fillet 1, sliced
spring onions 2, sliced
coriander leaves a small handful,
    chopped
red chilli 1, finely chopped
cheddar 50g, grated
salad leaves to serve

■ Put one tortilla in a heated, non-stick frying pan. Scatter over half the chicken, spring onion, coriander, chilli and cheese. Cover with another tortilla and flip to brown both sides. Repeat to make another quesadilla then cut into wedges and serve with salad. **Serves 2**

Serve these with a dollop of soured cream and some spicy tomato salsa for dipping.

Braised chicken with olives and tomatoes

30 minutes

rosemary 1 sprig, chopped
onion 1 large, sliced
garlic 2 cloves, sliced
new potatoes 500g small, quartered
olive oil
chicken pieces 8–10 thighs and
    drumsticks, skin on
baby plum or cherry tomatoes 500g
dry white wine 300ml
chicken stock fresh, cube or concentrate,
    made up to 300ml
kalamata olives 150g, drained
basil leaves a small bunch

■ Heat the oven to 220C/fan 200C/gas 7. Toss the first 4 ingredients in a roasting tray in 2 tbsp oil and cook for 25 minutes. Fry the chicken in 2 tbsp oil until browned and almost cooked through. Add to the tray for the last 10 minutes of cooking along with the tomatoes, wine, stock and the olives. Scatter with basil and serve.

Serves 4

To test chicken for doneness, pierce with a knife in the thickest part; the juices should run completely clear.

Creamy chicken and mushroom pies

30 minutes

---

butter 25g

spring onions 2 bunches, finely sliced

chestnut or **button mushrooms** 150g, quartered

shiitake mushrooms 150g, halved

flour 1 tbsp

milk 250ml

double cream 142ml carton

cooked chicken 1 small, torn into chunks, skin and bones discarded

tarragon leaves chopped to make 2 tbsp

ready-rolled puff pastry 1 sheet

egg 1, beaten

Most delis and supermarkets sell ready-roasted chickens or you could use packs of cooked breasts (you'll need 4 breasts for this).

■ Heat the oven to 220C/fan 200C/gas 7. Heat the butter in a large pan and cook the spring onion for a few minutes, then add the mushrooms and cook for 2 minutes.

■ Stir in the flour and cook for another minute, then gradually add the milk and cream and simmer until the sauce thickens. Stir in the chicken and tarragon.

■ Cut 4 circles from the pastry, big enough to cover 4 small pie dishes. Divide the chicken mixture between the dishes and brush the rims with beaten egg. Lift the pastry on to the pies, trimming off any excess. Press down and crimp the edges with a fork. Cut a couple of slits in the pastry to let out the steam and brush all over with the rest of the egg. Bake for 15–20 minutes, until the pastry is crisp and golden brown. **Serves 4**

Chilli chicken fajitas

30 minutes

olive oil for frying
chicken breasts 2 skinless, cut into strips
hot chilli powder 2 tsp
onion 1, halved and sliced
red pepper 1, sliced
green beans 100g
chopped tomatoes 400g tin
coriander leaves a handful, chopped
flour tortillas and **soured cream** to serve

■ Heat a couple of tablespoons of oil in a large pan. Throw in the chicken and quickly brown all over, then add the chilli powder and cook for a minute. Scoop out the chicken, then add the onion and red pepper to the pan and cook until softened. Tip in the green beans and tomatoes and return the chicken to the pan. Cover and simmer for 15 minutes. Stir through the coriander then drop the mixture into warm tortillas and roll up. Serve with a dollop of soured cream.

Serves 2

Chilli powder is a blend of different spices such as cayenne and cumin. Go for a milder version if you don't want it too hot.

Honey mustard chicken with herb salad

25 minutes

runny honey 2 tbsp
wholegrain mustard 1 tbsp
chicken breasts 2, skinless
herb salad 1 bag
cherry tomatoes 100g, halved
extra-virgin olive oil 2 tbsp
balsamic vinegar 1 tbsp

■ Mix the honey and mustard together, season and brush all over the chicken breasts. Grill the chicken for 5 minutes each side, until golden and cooked through, rest for 5 minutes then slice. Divide the salad, tomatoes and chicken between 2 plates. Whisk together the oil and balsamic and drizzle over. **Serves 2**

Leaving the skin off the chicken makes this a healthier option, but leaving it on gives you a crisper result.

Lemon and caper chicken

15 minutes

oil and **butter** for frying
mini chicken fillets 350g pack (or use
 2 chicken breasts)
capers 2 tbsp
lemon 1, juiced
salad leaves to serve

■ Heat 1 tbsp oil and a knob of butter in a frying pan until sizzling. Add the chicken fillets and cook for 2–3 minutes on each side or until golden and cooked through. Throw in the capers and lemon juice and stir until warmed through. Serve on salad leaves. **Serves 2**

This recipe uses false fillets from the chicken breast (often sold as mini fillets in packs) but you can use 2 normal chicken breasts instead that have been butterflied (slit horizontally and opened out like a book).

Soy and ginger chicken

20 minutes

pak choi 1 large head, quartered
skinless chicken breasts 2
root ginger a small piece, grated
garlic 1 clove, crushed
soy sauce 1 tbsp
rice wine, mirin or **dry sherry** 1 tbsp
spring onions 2, chopped into lengths
Tilda Rizazz brown basmati 1 pack

■ Put the pak choi on a plate that will fit inside a steamer basket. Put the chicken on top and add the ginger, garlic, soy sauce, rice wine and spring onions. Bring a pan of water to the boil and set the steamer basket on top with the plate inside. Cover and steam for 6–8 minutes or until the chicken is cooked through.
■ Heat the rice according to packet instructions. Serve with the chicken, pak choi and any juices. **Serves 2**

Ready-cooked microwaveable rice is a great storecupboard standby as it only takes a couple of minutes to make up.

Dead good spaghetti carbonara

20 minutes

spaghetti 250g
butter for frying
shallot 1, finely chopped
garlic 2 cloves, finely chopped
smoked streaky bacon 6 rashers, chopped
eggs 2
single cream 142ml carton
parmesan 25g, finely grated

■ Boil a large pan of water and cook the pasta following the packet instructions. Meanwhile, heat a knob of butter in a small frying pan and cook the shallot, garlic and bacon for 5–7 minutes until golden. Beat together the eggs, cream, most of the parmesan and plenty of ground black pepper.

■ Drain the spaghetti and return to the pan, off the heat. Add the shallot and egg mixtures and toss together until the pasta is evenly coated. Divide between two bowls then scatter the rest of the parmesan over. Serve with a grinding of black pepper. **Serves 2**

Buy parmesan in one big piece and grate it yourself for the best flavour.

Pork chops with mustard and shallot sauce

30 minutes

olive oil for frying

pork chops 4, fat cut off if you prefer

shallots 6, thinly sliced

red wine vinegar 2 tbsp

white wine a small glass

wholegrain mustard 2 tbsp

low-fat crème fraîche 3 tbsp

green beans steamed, to serve

■ Heat a little oil in a non-stick frying pan. Season the chops then fry for about 4 minutes on each side and remove. Tip the shallots into the pan and cook for about 5 minutes, keep warm. Add the vinegar and reduce for a few more minutes then add the wine and cook for a couple of minutes. Stir in the mustard and crème fraîche and bubble away until thickened. Serve with the pork chops and green beans. **Serves 4**

If leaving the fat on, snip through it before cooking the pork chops to stop them curling up in the pan.

Steak with Spanish tomato salad

20 minutes

sirloin steaks 2
smoked paprika 1 tsp
olive oil
small red onion ½, sliced into half moons
cherry tomatoes 200g
coriander leaves small bunch, roughly chopped
red wine vinegar ½ tsp

■ Rub the steaks on both sides with half the paprika and 1 tbsp of olive oil. Season and then grill or fry for 2 minutes on each side. Rest for 5 minutes before slicing into strips. Combine the onion, tomatoes, coriander, remaining paprika and 1 tbsp olive oil, vinegar and some seasoning. Mix well and toss through the steaks.

Serves 2

Smoked paprika gives a very characteristic smoky flavour, but you could use ordinary paprika instead.

Spiced yoghurt pork with couscous

25 minutes

natural yoghurt 150ml
garam masala 2 tsp
garlic 1 clove, crushed
lemon 1, zested and juiced
pork loin chops 2
couscous 150g
chicken stock fresh, cube or concentrate, made up to 200ml, hot
coriander leaves a small bunch, roughly chopped

■ Mix together the yoghurt, garam masala, garlic, lemon zest and ½ the lemon juice. Season. Add the pork chops and marinate for 10 minutes.

■ Put the couscous in a bowl and pour the hot stock over. Cover and leave for 5 minutes. Fluff up with a fork, then stir in the coriander and remaining lemon juice. Grill the chops for 5 minutes each side or until golden and cooked through. Serve with the couscous. **Serves 2**

Pork chops can vary quite a lot in thickness – if yours are thick-cut give them an extra minute or so on each side.

Beef skewers with Asian salad

20 minutes

Chinese five-spice powder 1 tsp
vegetable oil
sweet chilli sauce
rump steak 250g, cut into strips
clear honey 1 tsp
white wine vinegar 1 tsp
Thai fish sauce (nam pla)
garlic 1 clove, crushed
salad leaves small bag
cucumber ½, halved, seeds scooped out and sliced
spring onions 3, finely sliced
dry roasted peanuts 50g, chopped
mint leaves a handful

■ Heat a ridged griddle pan or grill to very hot. Mix the five-spice, 1 tbsp vegetable oil and a few drops of chilli sauce in a bowl. Add the meat and stir until coated. Thread the strips on to metal or bamboo skewers (soak bamboo skewers in cold water for 20 minutes first), and griddle or grill for 2–3 minutes on each side until cooked through.

■ Meanwhile, mix the honey, vinegar, 1½ tbsp fish sauce, garlic, a few drops of chilli sauce and 2 tbsp oil in a small bowl. Mix the salad leaves, cucumber, spring onions and peanuts and toss with the dressing. Rip the mint leaves and add to the salad. Divide the skewers between 2 plates and serve with the salad and a little bowl of fish sauce mixed with chilli sauce for dipping. **Serves 2**

Thai fish sauce is made from fermented small fish, such as anchovies. Use it to add a deeply savoury, salty flavour to Asian dishes.

Tandoori-style lamb cutlets

30 minutes + marinating

lamb cutlets 8–12, well trimmed

root ginger 2 tsp, grated

garlic 3 cloves

green chilli 1 large, chopped and seeded if you don't like heat

coriander leaves chopped to make 4 tbsp

lemon ½, juiced

natural yoghurt 125g

tomato purée 1 tbsp

garam masala 1 tbsp

■ Bash the cutlets between layers of clingfilm until slightly flattened. Mix the marinade ingredients and put in a polythene bag with the cutlets. Make sure they are coated thoroughly and marinate for at least 1 hour in the bag.

■ Cook the lamb cutlets over a really hot part of the barbecue for 3 minutes on each side, so they are still a bit pink in the middle but blackened around the edges. Serve 2–3 per person. **Serves 4**

If it's not barbecue weather, just grill or griddle these chops on a very high heat instead.

Blackened lamb with peppers

30 minutes

butter 50g, melted
lamb cutlets 12
red onions 2 large, sliced into thick
    wedges
red peppers 2, sliced
flat-leaf parsley leaves a handful
lemon wedges to serve

SPICE MIX
cayenne 1 tsp
garlic granules ½ tsp
paprika 1 tsp
ground white pepper 1 tsp
dried thyme 1 tsp

■ Mix the butter with the spice mix ingredients. Season and then brush liberally all over both sides of the cutlets. Leave for at least 20 minutes.
■ Grill the onions and peppers until tender and starting to char at the edges.
■ Barbecue the lamb cutlets for 2–3 minutes on each side for medium cooking. Serve with the vegetables sprinkled with parsley and wedges of lemon. **Serves 4**

Make cutlets thinner by bashing them between sheets of clingfilm so they cook through quicker.

Chilli pork chops with coleslaw

30 minutes

pork chops 4 large or 8 small
mild chilli powder 2 tsp
olive oil 100ml
caster sugar 3 tbsp
cider vinegar 3 tbsp
mustard seeds ½ tsp
cabbage 1 small **red** or **green** or a mix
    of both, shredded
red onion 1 small, sliced

■ Sprinkle the pork chops on both sides with the chilli, 1 tbsp olive oil, 1 tbsp sugar. Season. Heat the rest of the sugar and olive oil with the vinegar, mustard seeds and seasoning in a small pan until the sugar has dissolved. Cook for a couple of minutes then set aside to cool slightly.
■ Put the cabbage and onion in a bowl. Pour the warm dressing over and mix. Grill or barbecue the chops for 5 minutes each side. Serve with the coleslaw.

Serves 4

Black and yellow mustard seeds are widely available, use either in this recipe.

Balsamic lamb chops with pea purée

20 minutes

lamb chops 6
balsamic vinegar 3 tbsp
extra-virgin olive oil 5 tbsp
mint leaves a small bunch, chopped
frozen peas 300g
parmesan grated to make 2 tbsp

■ Marinate the chops in 2 tbsp balsamic vinegar, 2 tbsp oil, half the mint and some seasoning. Meanwhile, cook the peas in boiling water for 2 minutes. Drain, then tip into a food processor and purée with the remaining mint, vinegar, olive oil, parmesan and some salt. Pour into a saucepan to reheat. Grill the chops for 2–3 minutes each side, then rest for 5 minutes in foil. Serve with the pea purée.
Serves 2

Keep your absolute best balsamic for drizzling on salads, use a cheaper version for cooking.

Lamb cutlets with almond tabbouleh

20 minutes

bulghar wheat 100g
flaked almonds 50g, roughly chopped
garlic 1 clove, crushed
mint leaves 1 bunch, chopped
plum tomatoes 2, chopped
lemon 1, juiced
olive oil
lamb cutlets 4–6

■ Put the bulghar wheat in a pan with plenty of water, bring to the boil and simmer for 2 minutes. Turn off the heat and leave to soak for 8 minutes.

■ Drain well, then stir in the almonds, garlic, mint and tomatoes. Season with salt, pepper and lemon juice. Brush the lamb cutlets with oil, season and grill or fry for 3 minutes on each side or until they are cooked how you like them.

Serves 2

Find bulghar wheat in the supermarket in the same aisle as couscous and rice.

Stir-fried sesame pork

30 minutes

pork tenderloin fillet 1, trimmed and cut
  into strips
sesame seeds 2 tbsp
oil for frying
stir-fry vegetables 1 packet, about 350g
pak choi 2 heads, leaves separated and
  large ones halved
soy sauce for dressing
sweet chilli sauce for dressing
lime 1, juiced

■ Roll the pork strips in the sesame
seeds. Heat a little oil in a wok and when
it is hot, stir-fry the pork until browned.
Tip onto a plate. Add the stir-fry
vegetables and pak choi to the wok and
stir-fry for a minute or 2 until almost
tender. Season with soy sauce, sweet
chilli sauce and lime juice – as much as
you like – then stir in the pork. Toss
everything together and serve as it is or
with rice or noodles. **Serves 4**

Sesame seeds burn quite easily, so keep a
close eye on the pan when cooking.

Beef and caramelized onion sandwiches with horseradish

30 minutes

olive oil 4 tbsp

onions 2 large, finely sliced

sirloin or rump steaks 4, about 200g each

crème fraîche 100g

grated horseradish 4 tbsp, or 4 tbsp
    horseradish sauce

lemon juice a squeeze

watercress 100g

crusty rolls or mini ciabattas 8, halved

■ Heat the olive oil in a frying pan. Add the onion and season. Cook on a medium heat for 10–15 minutes until golden and caramelized.

■ Season the steaks well then barbecue or griddle (chargrill) for 2–3 minutes each side for rare or medium, then rest for 10 minutes.

■ Mix together the crème fraîche, horseradish, lemon juice and season. Slice the meat to about 1 cm thick. Fill each bread roll with steak, watercress, onions and horseradish cream and serve.

Serves 8

Fresh horseradish can vary in strength, so add more or less depending on which one you buy.

Pork with five-spice, walnuts and green beans

30 minutes

pork tenderloin fillet about 500g
Chinese five-spice 1 tsp
olive oil for frying
walnuts 50g
green beans 300g
shallot 1, finely chopped
white wine vinegar

■ Slice the pork loin into thin medallions. Season well and rub in a pinch of Chinese five-spice. Heat a little oil in a frying pan and add the pork. Fry on both sides until lightly browned then add the walnuts and fry for another couple of minutes.

■ Meanwhile, cook the beans for 3 minutes or until just tender, rinse under cold running water and then drain. Toss with the shallot, a little olive oil and a drizzle of vinegar. Pile the beans onto 2 plates and then spoon over the pork and walnuts. **Serves 4**

You could use mange tout or sugar snaps in place of the green beans.

Lamb and cherry tomatoes with lemon couscous

20 minutes

couscous 150g

lemon 1, zested and juiced

butter

chicken stock fresh, cube or concentrate,
    made up to 200ml, hot

lamb leg steaks 2

cherry tomatoes 250g

olive oil

mint leaves a small handful

■ Put the couscous in a bowl with the lemon zest and a knob of butter. Pour the hot stock over, cover with clingfilm and leave to swell.

■ Heat a solid frying pan to very hot. Brush the steaks with oil and season. Fry for 2–3 minutes each side then rest under foil. Tip the cherry tomatoes into the hot pan with a drop of olive oil and some seasoning and cook until they start to soften and blister (but still have some shape). Stir the mint and a little lemon juice through the couscous and serve with the lamb, tomatoes and any juices.

Serves 2

Add a pinch of dried chilli flakes to the cherry tomatoes when cooking to spice things up a bit.

Stir-fry beef and broccoli with oyster sauce

20 minutes

oil for frying

rump steaks 2, trimmed of fat and sliced into strips

spring onions 6, sliced

root ginger a thumb-sized piece, finely chopped

garlic 1 clove, finely chopped

Tenderstem broccoli 200g, blanched for 2 minutes

oyster sauce 4 tbsp

red chilli 1, finely sliced

■ Heat a little oil in a wok or large frying pan and quickly brown the steak all over. Scoop out, then tip in two-thirds of the spring onions, the ginger and garlic and cook for 2 minutes. Add the beef with the broccoli, oyster sauce and a splash of water. Cover and cook for 3–4 minutes. Scatter the rest of the spring onions and the chilli over. Serve with steamed basmati rice. **Serves 2**

Tenderstem broccoli are perfect for stir-frying as you can eat the whole stem and it needs no trimming.

Grilled veal with lemon and paprika

20 minutes

veal escalopes 2, bashed until thin
olive oil
paprika ½ tsp, smoked or ordinary
lemon 1, quartered
green salad to serve

■ Heat the grill to high. Line a baking sheet with non-stick baking parchment. Rub the veal with a little oil, season and dust with paprika. Lay the veal and lemon quarters on the baking tray and grill on both sides for about 2 minutes or until the veal is browned and cooked. Serve with the lemon and green salad. **Serves 2**

Choose welfare-friendly rose veal which is now available from larger supermarkets and good butchers.

Baked eggs with ham and tomato

20 minutes

olive oil for frying

garlic 1 clove, chopped

chopped tomatoes 400g tin

basil leaves a few, shredded

cooked ham 4 slices, roughly torn

eggs 2

crusty bread to serve

■ Heat the oven to 180C/fan 160C/gas 4. Heat a little oil in a pan, sizzle the garlic for a few seconds then add the tomatoes and simmer for 10 minutes until thickened.

■ Stir in the basil. Divide the sauce and ham between 2 individual baking dishes. Crack an egg on top and season. Bake for 12–14 minutes until just set. Serve with crusty bread. **Serves 2**

You could top these with a layer of grated cheese before baking for a richer finish.

Sausages grilled with tomato and sage

30 minutes

chipolata sausages 6
onion 1 small, sliced
chopped tomatoes 400g tin
sage leaves a small handful, chopped
sweet potatoes 3, peeled and cut
　　into chunks
olive oil

■ Heat the grill. Put the sausages in a shallow, ovenproof dish with the onion and grill for 10 minutes, turning the sausages occasionally. Add the tomatoes and sage. Season and stir well. Grill again for 10 minutes or until the tomatoes start to brown around the edges.

■ Meanwhile, boil the sweet potato until just tender, about 7–8 minutes, then roughly crush with a little olive oil and seasoning. Serve with the sausages.

Serves 2

Look for free-range pork chipolatas which are now widely available.

Prawn and pea risotto

30 minutes

butter for frying
olive oil
onion 1 small, finely chopped
garlic 2 cloves, crushed
carnaroli or **arborio rice** 300g
white wine 100ml (optional)
vegetable stock fresh, cube or
   concentrate, made up to 800ml
cooked peeled prawns 250g, defrosted
   if frozen
frozen peas 100g, defrosted
parmesan 80g, grated

■ Melt a knob of butter with a dash of olive oil in a wide shallow pan and add the onion. Cook until softened, then add the garlic and cook for a minute but don't brown. Tip in the rice and mix well. Add the wine (if using) and stir till it evaporates. Pour in enough stock to just cover the rice and gently simmer, stirring now and again. As the stock evaporates and the rice swells, add more stock and stir until all of it is used up; this will take about 12–15 minutes. Finally, add the prawns and the peas and season. Simmer for 2 minutes, mix in half the parmesan just before serving, then sprinkle the remainder over the top.

Serves 4

Look for carnaroli or arborio rice rather than just regular risotto rice, as they give a better result.

Moroccan tuna kebabs with couscous

20 minutes

tuna steaks 2, cut into large chunks

harissa 2 tbsp, plus extra to serve

lemons 2, 1 juiced, 1 cut into wedges

vegetable stock fresh, cube or
   concentrate, made up to 200ml, hot,
   mixed with 1 tsp **ground cumin**

couscous 100g

wooden skewers 4, soaked in water for
   30 minutes

mint leaves a small bunch, roughly
   chopped

■ Toss the tuna with the harissa and 2 tbsp lemon juice and leave for 10 minutes. Pour the stock over the couscous. Cover, leave for 5 minutes, then fluff with a fork. Thread the tuna on to 4 skewers and grill for a minute each side. Mix the rest of the lemon juice and the mint with the couscous. Serve with the tuna kebabs, lemon wedges and a little extra harissa. **Serves 2**

Look for thick-cut tuna steaks or buy about 300g tuna in one piece from the fishmonger's and cut it yourself.

Salmon cakes with lemon mayo

20 minutes

mashed potato 200g (use leftovers or buy ready-made)

tinned red salmon 200g, bones and skin removed

spring onions 2, finely sliced

egg 1, beaten

flour

breadcrumbs 4 tbsp

oil for frying

mayonnaise 3 tbsp mixed with ½ tbsp **lemon juice**

■ Mix the mash, salmon and spring onions with half the egg. Season. Shape the mixture into 4 small cakes. Dust with flour then dip into the remaining egg and then the breadcrumbs. Rest for 5 minutes in the fridge. Fry gently in oil for 3–4 minutes each side until golden. Serve with the lemon mayo and salad. **Serves 2**

This recipe would also work well with tinned tuna.

Mussels with coriander cream

30 minutes

mussels 2kg, cleaned and any beards
    removed
butter
red onion 1, finely chopped
garlic 4 cloves, finely chopped
white wine
single cream 142ml pot
coriander leaves a large handful, roughly
    chopped

■ Throw away any broken mussels or open ones that don't close after a tap on the sink. Melt a large knob of butter in a large saucepan and cook the onion and garlic for a minute or two until transparent and soft. Turn up the heat, tip in the mussels with a good slosh of wine then cover and cook for 3 minutes or until all the shells have opened – throw away any that haven't. Pour in the cream and stir well, throw in the coriander, season and serve in large bowls. **Serves 6**

For a Thai-style dish, add a teaspoon of green curry paste to the onion and garlic and substitute coconut milk for the single cream.

Prawn skewers with peanut dipping sauce

30 minutes

large raw prawns 1 kg with shell on
(about 30)

oil 2 tbsp

ground coriander 1 tbsp

ground cumin 1 tbsp

turmeric a large pinch

palm sugar or **soft light brown sugar**
100g

red chillies 2 small, finely sliced

kaffir lime leaves 4, finely shredded
(optional) or zest of 1 lime

roasted unsalted peanuts 5 tbsp,
finely chopped

cucumber ¼, seeded and finely chopped

■ Peel the middle body section of the prawn shells, leaving the tail and head intact. Skewer 3–4 prawns on to 8 metal skewers.

■ Mix the oil, coriander, cumin, turmeric and a little salt together. Brush the mixture all over the prawn skewers. Chill for at least 1 hour to marinate.

■ Meanwhile, heat the sugar with 125ml water in a small saucepan, stir until the sugar dissolves then bring to the boil. Add the chillies and kaffir lime leaves, cover and cool to room temperature before stirring through the peanuts and cucumber.

■ Barbecue the skewers for about 3–4 minutes each side, turning once, until cooked through. Serve immediately with a little dipping sauce spooned over and the remaining sauce served in a small dish. **Serves 4**

Kaffir lime leaves are available from Thai shops and some greengrocers and delis.

Prawn and ginger noodle salad

20 minutes

fine rice noodles 250g pack

large prawns 250g, peeled and cooked

mango 1 small, peeled and sliced

light soy sauce 4 tbsp

root ginger 2-inch piece, finely grated

lime 1, juiced

coriander leaves a large bunch, roughly
chopped

■ Soak the noodles in boiling water for
6–7 minutes, until tender. Rinse under
cold running water then drain and put in
a bowl with the prawns and mango.

■ Whisk the soy sauce with the ginger,
lime juice and some black pepper and
pour over the noodles. Scatter the
coriander over and toss together. **Serves 4**

Use a micrograter to get the best results
when grating ginger.

Glazed salmon with mustard dill sauce

20 minutes

Dijon mustard 5 tbsp
dill leaves a small bunch, chopped
soft light brown sugar 4 tbsp
salmon fillets 4, skinless
lemon juice 1 tbsp
cider vinegar or **white wine vinegar**
    1 tbsp

■ Heat the grill. In a small bowl mix 2 tbsp mustard, half the dill, and 2 tbsp sugar. Coat the salmon fillets with the mixture, season, then grill for 6–7 minutes until glazed and cooked through.

■ Mix the remaining mustard, dill and brown sugar with the lemon juice and vinegar to make a sauce. Serve with the salmon and a salad. **Serves 4**

You could use wholegrain mustard for this, but don't be tempted to try English mustard – it would be too overpowering.

Baked fish with parsley mayo

30 minutes

Jersey Royal or **new potatoes** 500g, halved

cherry tomatoes 200g, halved

olive oil

white fish fillets 4, halved

lemon 1, ½ sliced, ½ juiced

capers 2 tbsp

mayonnaise 200g

flat-leaf parsley leaves a small bunch, finely chopped

■ Heat the oven to 200C/fan 180C/gas 6. Put the potatoes and tomatoes on a large baking tray, drizzle with olive oil and season. Roast for 20 minutes then add the fish, top with lemon slices and a few capers and cook for 8–10 minutes.

■ Meanwhile, mix the mayonnaise, parsley, lemon juice and remaining capers in a bowl and season. Serve with the fish and potatoes. **Serves 4**

Look for capers packed in salt – chefs swear by them – but make sure you rinse them really well before use.

Trout with watercress sauce

30 minutes

rainbow trout fillets 2
watercress 100g, roughly chopped
low-fat fromage fraîs 200g tub
capers 2 tbsp, rinsed and chopped
lemon ½, juiced
iceberg lettuce ½, cut into wedges

■ Heat the oven to 180C/fan 160C/gas 4. Put the trout fillets on a piece of oiled foil, season and fold up to make a parcel. Cook for 10–15 minutes or until the flesh looks opaque. Meanwhile, whiz the watercress with the fromage fraîs in a blender or food processor. Stir in the capers and lemon juice, season. Serve the trout and iceberg wedges with the watercress sauce. **Serves 2**

You could also cook the trout fillets in a steamer basket on top of the stove.

Grilled salmon with lemon courgettes

30 minutes

small salad potatoes 2 handfuls, skin on
olive oil for frying
courgettes 2, sliced
garlic 1 clove, crushed
lemon 1, zested and juiced
basil leaves 2 handfuls
salmon fillets 2, skin on

■ Boil the potatoes for 15 minutes until tender. Drain, cool a little and halve. Heat ½ tbsp olive oil in a separate pan and add the courgettes. Stir and fry for 3 minutes until they start to brown at the edges. Add the garlic and lemon zest and cook until fragrant. Season and add the lemon juice – the courgettes should be very lemony. Stir through the basil and potato halves.

■ Meanwhile, heat a non-stick pan with a little oil. Cook the salmon fillets skin-side down for about 5 minutes, until the skin is golden brown and crisp, then turn over and cook for 1 minute. Serve the courgettes with the salmon. **Serves 2**

Use Jersey Royals for this when in season, as they have a lovely buttery flavour.

Salmon with lemon pesto crust

30 minutes

white breadcrumbs a handful
lemon 1, ½ zested and juiced, ½ cut
    into wedges
pesto 2 tbsp
salmon fillets 2, skinless
Tenderstem broccoli to serve
olive oil

■ Heat the oven to 220C/fan 200C/gas 7. Mix the breadcrumbs with a little lemon zest and the pesto, then press the mixture all over the top of the salmon fillets. Bake for 10–12 minutes until the crust is turning golden and the salmon is just cooked. Steam the broccoli for 4 minutes then dress with a little olive oil and lemon juice. Dress the salmon with the lemon wedges and serve together with the broccoli. **Serves 2**

Buy pesto fresh in tubs from the chiller cabinet.

Seared salmon with lime aïoli and watercress

20 minutes

olive oil for frying
salmon fillets 2, seasoned
limes 2, 1 zested and juiced, 1 halved
mayonnaise 4 tbsp, good quality
garlic 1 clove, crushed
watercress 2 large handfuls

■ Heat a little olive oil in a frying pan and cook the salmon fillets on both sides until they are browned and cooked through.

■ Meanwhile, add enough lime juice and zest to the mayonnaise along with the garlic to give it flavour without making it too sloppy. Add the remaining juice to the salmon in the pan. Season. Serve the salmon with the lime aïoli and watercress. **Serves 2**

Look for mayonnaise made with organic eggs for the best flavour.

Lemon sole with flageolet beans

20 minutes

red onion ½, finely chopped
plum tomatoes 3, quartered
parsley leaves chopped to make 4 tbsp
flageolet beans 1 tin, drained and rinsed
olive oil
lemon 1, ½ juiced, ½ cut into wedges
lemon sole fillets 4 small, or 2 large
butter

■ Mix the onion, tomatoes, parsley and beans in a bowl. Add a slug of olive oil and squeeze half the lemon over.

■ Heat a little olive oil in a large frying pan and add the fillets, skin-side down. Fry quickly until browned on the bottom then leave over a gentle heat for a few minutes with the lid on to cook through. Spoon some of the oil over and add a knob of butter. Serve with the beans and tomatoes and a wedge of lemon. **Serves 2**

Cannellini or borlotti beans would also work well here.

Fish curry

30 minutes

onion 1, finely sliced

olive oil for frying

curry paste 2 tbsp (Madras is good for this)

chopped tomatoes 2 × 400g tins

white fish fillets 450g, cut into large chunks

coriander leaves a small handful

naan bread or basmati rice to serve

■ Fry the onion in a large pan with a little oil until softened then add the curry paste and cook for 2 minutes. Stir in the tomatoes and simmer for 10 minutes until reduced and thickened. Add the fish and gently simmer for 3–4 minutes until the fish is cooked through. Scatter with coriander and serve with naan bread or steamed basmati rice. **Serves 4**

Use sustainable firm, white fish for this. For an up-to-date list of safe fish to eat visit fishonline.org.

Roast cod with salsa verde

30 minutes

olive oil

cod (buy line-caught Pacific) or other
  firm **white fish** 6 pieces of fillet
  about 175g each, skin on

SALSA VERDE

flat-leaf parsley leaves from a small
  bunch

mint leaves from a small bunch

capers 3 tbsp, rinsed and drained

garlic 1 clove, crushed

Dijon mustard 1 tbsp

extra-virgin olive oil 125ml

■ Heat the oven to 220C/fan 200C/gas 7.
Oil a non-stick baking sheet and put it
in the oven to heat up – this will help the
skin crisp up. Put the pieces of cod on to
the hot baking sheet, skin-side down.
Season and put them in the oven for
8 minutes.

■ Meanwhile, whiz the ingredients for
the salsa verde in a food processor,
adding the oil in batches until you have a
thick but spoonable sauce. Season. Serve
the cod skin-side up with the salsa verde
and some salad. **Serves 6**

The salsa verde recipe is really versatile
– you can also serve it with chargrilled
steaks, roast pork or chicken.

Salmon, fennel and herb parcels

30 minutes

---

fennel 2 small bulbs, halved and
    finely sliced
salmon 4 fillets
cherry tomatoes 16, halved
rosemary leaves from 2 sprigs, chopped
dry white wine
green beans steamed, to serve

■ Heat the oven to 200C/fan 180C/gas 6. Tear 4 large sheets of foil. Divide the fennel between them, sit a salmon fillet on each then scatter the tomatoes and rosemary over and add a splash of wine. Scrunch up the foil to make 4 parcels, put on a baking tray then cook for 10–15 minutes until just cooked through – you'll have to open a parcel to check. Serve with green beans. **Serves 4**

This also makes a great barbecue dish as the parcels can go straight on the grill, but wait until the coals have died down a bit.

Soba noodles with prawns, broccoli and mushrooms

20 minutes

soba noodles 125g

chicken stock fresh, cube or concentrate, made up to 500ml

soy sauce 2 tbsp

broccoli 1 small head, cut into florets

shiitake or **button mushrooms** 8, sliced

North Atlantic prawns 125g

■ Cook the noodles in boiling water until they are al dente, about 3–4 minutes. Rinse and drain. Heat the chicken stock with the soy sauce to a simmer. Add the broccoli and cook for 2 minutes, then add the mushrooms and cook for 2 minutes more. Add the prawns and heat through. Divide the noodles between 2 large bowls and spoon the soup over. **Serves 2**

Find soba (buckwheat) noodles in larger supermarkets, health-food shops and Asian grocers, or use egg noodles.

Tuna steaks with chunky avocado salsa

20 minutes

tuna steaks 2, oiled and seasoned
tomatoes 2, chopped
avocado 1, chopped
red onion ½, finely chopped
chilli 1, seeded and finely chopped
lime 1, ½ juiced, ½ wedges
olive oil 1 tbsp
rocket 2 handfuls

■ Heat a griddle pan (chargrill) to high. Sear the tuna for 2 minutes on each side. Toss together the tomatoes, avocado, red onion and chilli with the lime juice and the olive oil, then fold through the rocket. Serve with the tuna and lime wedges.

Serves 2

Always oil fish well before griddling and make sure your griddle is blisteringly hot to avoid sticking.

Cauliflower cheese with crunchy sage topping

30 minutes

cauliflower 1, broken into pieces

leeks 4, trimmed

butter 50g

white bread 3 slices, crusts removed and roughly chopped

sage leaves 2 tbsp, chopped

Merchant Gourmet SunBlush tomatoes 50g, plus 3 tbsp oil from the pack

wholegrain mustard 2 tbsp

plain flour 3 tbsp

milk 400ml

Gruyère 100g, grated

■ Simmer the cauliflower for 8 minutes or until tender, then drain. Meanwhile, fry the leeks in the butter for 10 minutes until soft. Whiz the bread and sage to crumbs in a food processor. Add the tomatoes and their oil and whiz until chopped. Add the mustard and flour to the leeks and stir. Add a third of the milk and stir until thickened. Gradually add the rest of the milk and bring to a simmer. Stir in the cheese. Divide between 4 ovenproof dishes and pour the sauce over. Scatter the crumbs over and grill for 5 minutes.

Serves 4

Serving these in individual dishes makes it look a bit smarter, but cook it one big dish if you prefer.

Pear and dolcelatte salad

20 minutes

walnut bread 4–6 slices, cut into long triangles
olive oil
pears 6 small, halved
rocket 125g bag
dolcelatte 150g, pulled into pieces
pine nuts 50g, toasted
lemon 1, halved

■ Brush the walnut bread with a little oil and grill it until crisp on both sides. Heat a little oil in a frying pan and fry the pears cut-side down until they brown, then flip them over and cook the other side for a minute or two or until they start to soften. Divide the walnut toast between 4 shallow bowls and heap some rocket on top, then scatter the cheese and pine nuts over. Add 3 pear halves to each bowl and dress with more olive oil, a squeeze of lemon and seasoning.

Serves 4

Dolcelatte is a very creamy blue cheese – you could also use Roquefort or Gorgonzola.

Spring greens and blue cheese risotto

30 minutes

spring greens or **spinach** 500g, roughly chopped
olive oil 2 tbsp
butter
onion 1, finely chopped
garlic 2 cloves, finely chopped
risotto rice 400g
white wine 150ml
vegetable stock fresh, cube or concentrate, made up to 600ml, hot
flat-leaf parsley leaves chopped to make 4 tbsp
blue cheese (such as dolcelatte) 150g, crumbled
pine nuts 25g, toasted

Make sure the risotto is off the heat before you add the cheese. You don't want it to melt into the rice completely.

■ Boil 600ml water with a pinch of salt and cook the greens for 1 minute. Drain, reserving the liquid.

■ Heat a large pan and add the oil and a small knob of butter. Heat until the butter is foaming then add the onion and gently cook for a couple of minutes until softened. Add the garlic and cook for a minute. Stir in the rice until the grains are shiny and coated. Pour in the wine and cook over a high heat until it has evaporated.

■ Turn down the heat to medium and begin to add the liquid from the spring greens, a ladleful at a time, allowing it to be absorbed into the rice before adding more. When the liquid is used up, continue the process with the stock. It should take about 20 minutes.

■ When the texture is creamy but each grain is still firm to the bite in the centre, the risotto is ready. Take it off the heat and stir in the greens, parsley, blue cheese and pine nuts. Season. Leave to rest with the lid on for a few minutes then serve immediately. **Serves 4**

Radicchio and halloumi salad with lemon anchovy dressing

20 minutes

halloumi 250g pack, drained and sliced
olive oil 2 tbsp
garlic 1 clove, finely chopped
anchovies 2, rinsed and finely chopped
lemon ½, zested and juiced
sourdough or **brown bread** 3 thick slices
radicchio ½ head, ripped into pieces
parsley small bunch, finely chopped

■ Grill the halloumi on each side until golden. Heat the olive oil in a small pan, add the garlic and anchovies and cook until golden. Add the lemon zest and juice off the heat. Toast the bread in a toaster then cut into cubes. Divide the radicchio between 4 plates. Top with croutons, cheese and dressing, and sprinkle over the parsley. **Serves 4**

Halloumi is a hard, salty cheese which keeps its shape really well when grilled or fried.

Pea, feta and mint frittata

30 minutes

spring onions 6, finely chopped
olive oil for frying
eggs 6, lightly beaten and seasoned
feta 100g, broken into pieces
frozen peas 150g, defrosted
mint leaves small bunch, shredded

■ Heat the grill. Cook the spring onions in a little olive oil in a non-stick frying pan until softened. Add the eggs, feta, peas and mint, stir to combine then leave over the heat until the bottom has set. Slide under the grill to finish off. Serve cut into wedges. **Serves 2**

To quickly defrost peas, put them in a colander and pour over a kettle of boiling water.

Tagliatelle with watercress pesto

15 minutes

tagliatelle 200g

watercress 50g, any woody stalks
    removed

pine nuts 2 tbsp

olive oil 3 tbsp

lemon ½, juiced

garlic 1 clove

mozzarella 1 ball, torn into pieces

■ Cook the pasta according to the packet instructions. Whiz the rest of the ingredients (except the mozzarella) in a food processor. Drain the tagliatelle and toss the pesto through the pasta with the mozzarella. **Serves 2**

Watercress comes into season around May and will be young and less woody then, perfect for this recipe.

Loaded mushroom burgers

20 minutes

large flat mushrooms 8, stems trimmed
olive oil
tomatoes 3, diced
chilli 1 small, finely chopped
garlic 1 clove, finely chopped
red onion ½ small, finely chopped
ciabatta 4, or other crusty buns, toasted
salad leaves a handful
emmental 4 slices

■ Heat a griddle (chargrill) pan. Brush the mushrooms liberally with olive oil and season. Cook both sides for 3 minutes each. Mix together the tomatoes, chilli, garlic and onion with a slug of olive oil. Build the burgers between the toasted ciabatta or buns with layers of salad leaves, the mushrooms and cheese, and top with the tomato salsa. **Serves 4**

Mushrooms are like sponges for soaking up flavour so try brushing with lemon or chilli oil before grilling.

Griddled asparagus, pea and feta salad

15 minutes

asparagus 150g, trimmed

olive oil 3 tbsp, plus a little extra

frozen peas 200g

feta 100g, broken into chunks

lemon juice 1 tbsp

basil and/or **mint leaves** from a small bunch, chopped (keep a few leaves whole to serve)

■ Brush the asparagus with olive oil and griddle (chargrill) until tender. Boil the peas for 2 minutes then drain. Make the dressing by whisking 3 tbsp olive oil with the lemon juice. Toss together with the other ingredients then sprinkle with the reserved basil and mint leaves. **Serves 2**

Asparagus comes in a variety of colours, so liven up this dish with green, purple or white asparagus.

Spinach and sweet potato curry

30 minutes

onion 1, finely sliced

Madras curry paste 2–3 tbsp, depending on how hot you like your curry

coconut milk 400g tin

sweet potatoes 2 orange-fleshed ones, cut into chunks

spinach 200g, washed and roughly chopped

naan breads 4, warmed through

■ Fry the onion until very soft, about 8 minutes. Stir in the paste and fry for 2 minutes. Add the coconut milk and sweet potatoes and cook until just tender, about 10 minutes. Stir through the spinach until wilted. Serve with naan bread. **Serves 4**

Use half-fat coconut milk for this if you want a lighter result.

Eggs Florentine

30 minutes

eggs 6, fresh as possible
olive oil
young spinach 400g
muffins 6, split and toasted

HOLLANDAISE
egg yolks 4
lemon juice 2 tbsp
unsalted butter 200g

Serve this in a large dish rather than cooking each one to order and you'll be able to sit down and enjoy it with everyone else.

■ Bring a large frying pan of water to a simmer and break in the eggs carefully, one by one. Bring the water back to a simmer for 1 minute then turn the heat off and cover the pan for 10 minutes.

■ Heat a little oil in a pan and wilt the spinach. Season and keep warm.

■ To make the hollandaise, put the egg yolks in a blender with the lemon juice. Melt the butter in a small pan until it has separated into a clear yellow liquid and some white sediment. Start the blender and then pour in the clear melted butter through the top hole in a steady stream. Season.

■ Divide the spinach into piles in a warmed serving dish. Lift an egg onto each spinach pile with a slotted spoon (drain them well) and pour the hollandaise over the top. Put under the grill for a couple of minutes to brown the hollandaise, if you like. Serve with toasted muffins. **Serves 6**

Puy lentil salad with mozzarella

30 minutes

Puy lentils 225g
red onion 1, finely sliced
lemons 2, juiced
roasted red peppers 150g, sliced, from the deli or a jar
semi-dried (sun blushed) tomatoes 16
mozzarella 2 large balls, ripped into pieces, or 2 tubs of **bocconcini**
basil leaves a bunch
extra-virgin olive oil
mixed salad leaves 4 handfuls

■ Cook the lentils in simmering water for 20 minutes. Drain. Meanwhile, soak the red onion in half the lemon juice for 5 minutes. Once the lentils are cooked, add the drained onion, remaining lemon juice, peppers and tomatoes. Stir through the mozzarella and basil, season and dress with olive oil. Arrange some salad leaves on each plate and spoon some lentil salad into the centre. **Serves 4**

This salad is also lovely with goat's cheese or feta.

Watercress and taleggio risotto

30 minutes

vegetable stock fresh, cube or
    concentrate, made up to 1 ½ litres
unsalted butter
olive oil 1 tbsp
onion 1 small, chopped
arborio rice 325g
watercress a large bunch, about 100g,
    chopped
taleggio 125g, rind removed, chopped

■ Bring the stock to a simmer in a saucepan. Heat a small knob of butter and the olive oil in a wide saucepan. Add the onion and fry for 3 minutes. Add the rice and stir until all the grains are coated and shiny. Pour in a ladle of stock and stir until completely absorbed. Continue adding stock and stirring until the rice is tender with a little bite left to it. Add the watercress and taleggio. Remove from the heat, add another knob of butter and serve.

Serves 4

Taleggio is a semi-soft Italian cheese which melts really well – you can use brie instead if you prefer.

Penne with goat's cheese and walnuts

15 minutes

penne pasta 350g
soft goat's cheese or cream cheese
    with herbs 125g
walnuts 50g, roughly chopped
lemon 1, zested
chives a small bunch, snipped
rocket 100g

■ Cook the pasta according to packet instructions. Drain, reserving 2 tbsp cooking water, and return to the pan.

■ Stir the cheese, walnuts, lemon zest, chives and reserved cooking water through the pasta. Season, mix in the rocket (the heat of the pasta should be enough to wilt it) and serve. **Serves 4**

Use scissors to snip through chives rather than chopping on a board.

Halloumi with broad beans and artichokes

30 minutes

oil for frying

onion ½, finely chopped

broad beans 350g podded weight
(double-podded if you like and
have time)

peas 350g

cooked artichoke hearts in oil 4 small,
quartered

lemon 1, juiced

mint leaves a handful

halloumi 250g block, thickly sliced

crusty bread or couscous to serve

You can use frozen broad beans for this
when they are not in season.

■ Heat a little oil in a wide saucepan
and fry the onion until just soft but not
coloured. Add the other ingredients
except the mint and the halloumi, plus
2 tbsp water. Cover and simmer gently
for 5 minutes. Stir in the mint.

■ Meanwhile grill or fry the halloumi
slices until they are golden. Serve the
broad beans hot or cold with the
halloumi slices and crusty bread or some
plain couscous. Serves 4

Quick tortilla pizzas

20 minutes

flour tortillas 4
mozzarella 1 ball, sliced
pepperonata 1 jar, (Sacla do a good one)
    or use about 150g marinated
    roasted peppers
rocket 50g

■ Heat the oven to 200C/fan 180C/gas 6. Put the 4 tortillas on a large baking sheet, scatter the mozzarella over and some of the pepperonata and cook for 5–7 minutes until turning golden at the edges and the cheese is melting. Top with some rocket and drizzle with a little oil from the jar. Cut into wedges and serve.
Serves 2

Pepperonata is a mixture of peppers, onions and garlic cooked in olive oil and makes a great speedy pizza topping.

Courgette frittata

30 minutes

red onion 1 small, halved and sliced
courgettes 2 medium, sliced
olive oil for frying
eggs 6
mature cheddar 50g, grated

■ Fry the onion and courgettes gently in a little olive oil for 10 minutes until softened and turning golden. Beat the eggs then mix in the cheese and veg. Heat some oil in a small non-stick frying pan and pour in the egg mixture. Cook, moving the egg around until the base is set. Slide under a hot grill until puffed and golden. Cut into wedges and serve with a leafy salad. **Serves 2**

You can use any green veg for this frittata; broccoli, spinach or asparagus also work well.

Linguine with cherry tomatoes and goat's cheese

20 minutes

linguine 200g

cherry tomatoes 250g, halved

green olives a decent handful

capers 1 tbsp, rinsed

basil leaves 1 pack, roughly chopped

soft goat's cheese 50g

■ Cook the pasta following the packet instructions, drain.

■ Meanwhile, tip the tomatoes, olives, capers and basil into a bowl and season well. Tip in the pasta and toss to combine. Add the goat's cheese in blobs and toss once. **Serves 2**

Choose a soft goat's cheese without a rind for this dish.

Brie and spinach croissants

20 minutes

young leaf spinach 100g, washed
butter
garlic ½ clove, crushed
croissants 2, slit open lengthways
brie 6 thick slices

■ Heat the grill to high. Cook the spinach in a little butter, with the garlic, until wilted. Squeeze out any excess liquid. Lightly toast the croissants on the cut side then pile on the spinach and brie. Grill again until oozing, then fold together. **Serves 2**

If you are not vegetarian, you could make this a heartier brunch dish by adding some slices of crisp bacon.

Gooey school treacle sponge

30 minutes

golden syrup 6 overloaded, oozing tbsp
butter 100g, plus extra for the dish
sugar 100g
eggs 2
vanilla essence ½ tsp
self-raising flour 100g
custard to serve

■ Butter a 1-litre baking dish, and dollop the syrup in the bottom. Put the butter and sugar in a food processor and blitz until pale. Beat in the eggs one by one, then the vanilla. Add the flour and pulse until just mixed. Scrape into the dish, on top of the syrup.

■ Cover with clingfilm and microwave on medium for 7 ½ minutes until risen and spongy. Serve with lashings of custard.

Serves 6

You could also cook this in a conventional oven. Bake at 180C/fan 160C/gas 4 for 30 minutes until risen and golden.

Mango and passionfruit fool

20 minutes

mangoes 2, ripe, peeled
lime ½, juiced
Greek yoghurt 500g
passion fruit 2

■ Dice one mango and divide almost half of it between 4 small bowls or glasses, saving some for the topping.

■ Put the remaining mango in a blender or mini food processor with the lime juice, and whiz to a purée. Beat the yoghurt until smooth, then swirl in the mango purée.

■ Pour into the bowls on top of the diced mango, scatter with the remaining chopped mango and scoop the seeds of half a passion fruit onto each one. Cover and put in the fridge to chill until needed.

Serves 4

These can be made a day in advance and chilled – the yoghurt will thicken up overnight.

Sticky toffee bananas

10 minutes

medium bananas 3, peeled
butter 1 tsp
dark rum 1 tbsp
orange ½, juiced
golden syrup 1 tbsp
half-fat crème fraîche 2 tbsp
pumpkin seeds 1 tbsp

■ Cut the bananas into diagonal chunks. Melt the butter in a non-stick frying pan. Add the bananas and fry until they begin to brown, tossing once or twice. Take off the heat, add the rum, orange juice and golden syrup, then put back and bubble for 30 seconds, shaking the pan to coat the bananas in the sauce.

■ Divide the bananas between 2 plates and top with the crème fraîche and pumpkin seeds. **Serves 2**

If you don't have any dark rum, brandy or whiskey will also work.

Chocolate soufflés

30 minutes

dark chocolate 200g, chopped
butter 150g, cut into cubes, plus extra
    for the ramekins
eggs 6
sugar 175g
plain flour 125g

■ Heat the oven to 180C/fan 160C/gas 4. Butter 6 medium ramekins. Melt the chocolate with the butter in a bowl over simmering water or in a microwave. Beat the eggs with the sugar until they are very light and fluffy and then fold in the flour. Fold in the chocolate mixture.

■ Divide between the ramekins (put them in the fridge at this point if you are making ahead). Bake for 8–12 minutes. The soufflés should rise and form a firm crust but you want them still to be slightly runny in the middle. Serve with cream. **Serves 6**

These melting chocolate puddings are much sturdier than ordinary soufflés and will behave even if made ahead and stored in the fridge until you cook them.

Toffee banana puffs with chantilly cream

30 minutes

bananas 4 small
ready-rolled puff pastry 2 sheets
egg 1, beaten
unrefined demerara sugar
double cream 284ml carton
icing sugar 2tbsp
vanilla extract a few drops

■ Heat the oven to 200C/fan 180C/gas 6. Slice the bananas in half horizontally. Unroll the pastry and lay the banana halves on top, cut-side-up. Cut around each half, leaving a 2cm border. Put the banana pastries on a baking sheet and brush the borders with egg. Sprinkle the tops of the pastries with demerara sugar.

■ Bake for 15–20 minutes until the pastry is puffed and golden and the bananas are caramelized. Softly whip the cream, icing sugar and vanilla together. Serve two puffs per person with a dollop of cream.

Serves 4

Try adding a good slug of Baileys to the cream instead of the vanilla for a boozy finish.

Blueberry cheesecake pots

25 minutes

butter 25g
digestive biscuits 5
blueberries 150g
caster sugar 2 tbsp
mascarpone 250g tub
double cream 4 tbsp
icing sugar 4 tbsp
lemon 1, zested and juiced

■ Melt the butter and then whiz it in a food processor with the digestive biscuits. Press the mixture into the bottom of 4 glasses and chill.

■ Cook the blueberries with the caster sugar for 2–3 minutes, then cool. Mix the mascarpone, double cream, icing sugar, lemon juice and zest together. Make alternate layers of cheesecake and blueberry mix in each glass and serve.

Serves 4

Blueberries freeze well, so keep a bag of them in the freezer for when they are out of season.

Blueberry vanilla pancakes

30 minutes

plain flour 150g
baking powder 1 tsp
golden caster sugar 2 tbsp
egg 1, beaten
butter 25g, melted and cooled slightly
vanilla extract a few drops
milk 150ml
blueberries 100g

■ Mix the dry ingredients (except the blueberries) with a pinch of salt. Mix the egg, melted butter, vanilla and milk and whisk into the dry mix to make a thick batter. Stir in the blueberries. Heat a non-stick frying pan and fry large spoonfuls of the batter mix until little holes appear on the surface, flip and cook the other side till golden. **Serves 2**

Serve these pancakes with vanilla ice cream for pudding or drizzled with maple syrup for breakfast.

Blackberry fluff

20 minutes

blackberries 300g
caster sugar 1 tbsp
mascarpone 250g carton
vanilla extract ½ tsp
double cream 142ml carton

■ Heat the blackberries (keeping a few aside) gently with the sugar for a couple of minutes or until they give off juice. Whiz in a food processor then push through a fine sieve. Beat the mascarpone with a spoon until it is floppy then fold in the blackberry purée and the vanilla extract. In a separate bowl, loosely whip the cream then fold it into the blackberry mixture. Spoon into 4 dishes and decorate with blackberries.

Serves 4

Sieving the blackberries will give you a smooth purée with no seeds and is worth the extra effort.

Banoffi tarts

30 minutes

ready-rolled puff pastry 1 sheet, fresh or
frozen, or a 250g block rolled out

bananas 2, sliced

brown sugar 2 tbsp

vanilla ice cream to serve

Carnation caramel or **dulce de leche**
4 tbsp, warmed

dark chocolate shaved with a potato
peeler, to decorate

■ Heat the oven to 200C/fan 180C/gas 6.
Cut 4 circles about 10cm in diameter
from the pastry sheet, prick them gently
with a fork then lay on a non-stick baking
sheet. Divide the banana slices between
them (in a single layer), leaving a 1 ½cm
border around the edge of each and
sprinkle brown sugar over the bananas.

■ Bake for 20–25 minutes until the pastry
is puffed, golden and crisp. Top each puff
with a scoop of vanilla ice cream, spoon
over Carnation caramel or dulce de leche
and decorate with chocolate shavings.

Serves 4

You can make the pastry bases ahead
and re-heat them before serving with
the ice cream.

Pineapple with lime and chilli syrup

25 minutes

caster sugar 100g
red chillies 2–3, depending on how hot
   you want the syrup, finely chopped
lime 1, zested and juiced
pineapple 1, halved, cored and cut into
   wafer-thin slices

■ Put the caster sugar in a pan with 100ml water. Heat slowly until the sugar has dissolved, then add the chillies and boil until the liquid becomes syrupy. Cool. Add the lime zest and juice. Lay the pineapple slices on a plate and drizzle the syrup over. **Serves 4**

Add a whole star anise or a couple of allspice berries with the chilli flakes for a spicier syrup.

Summer berry fools

20 minutes

raspberries 200g
strawberries 200g, hulled
icing sugar, 3 tbsp
Greek yoghurt 500ml
rosewater 1 tsp (optional)
shortbread biscuits to serve

■ Whiz the berries in a food processor with the icing sugar. Sieve to get rid of the seeds if you like. Mix the yoghurt, rosewater (if using) and half the fruit purée. Swirl in the rest of the purée and spoon the mixture into 4 dishes. Chill until needed. Serve with shortbread.

Serves 4

You can use frozen, defrosted berries for this when they are not in season.

Lemon mousse

20 minutes

double cream 284ml carton
lemon 1, juiced and zested
caster sugar 60g
egg whites 2

■ Put the cream, lemon zest and sugar into a large bowl and whisk them together until the mixture starts to thicken. Add the lemon juice and whisk again until the mixture thickens further – but don't let it get too stiff or you won't be able to fold in the egg whites. Whisk the egg whites until they form soft peaks and then fold them into the lemon mixture. Spoon the mousse into 4 glasses and chill. Decorate with extra zest if you like. **Serves 4**

This light, palate-cleansing dessert is perfect served after a heavy main course.

Index

Picture credits and recipe credits

BBC Books and **olive** would like to thank the following for providing photographs. While every effort has been made to trace and acknowledge all photographers, we would like to apologise should there be any errors or omissions.

Iain Bagwell p63; Peter Cassidy p4, p13, p15, p25, p27, p35, p59, p119, p137, p161, p167, p169, p187, p191, p193, p199, p201; Jason Lowe p10, p49, p73, p77, p83, p85, p153, p155, p159; David Munns p4, p23, p93, p103, p125; Myles New p17, p19, p53, p91, p122, p124, p171, p195; Michael Paul p47, p78, p111, p113, p115, p147, p149, p151; William Reavell p52; Roger Stowell p69, p89; Debi Treloar p117; Simon Walton p4, p31, p33, p37, p51, p61, p67, p75, p87, p95, p97, p105, p107, p109, p121, p129, p131, p139, p141, p143, p163, p165, p175, p181, p183, p185; Philip Webb p197; Simon Wheeler p4, p6, p21, p29, p39, p41, p43, p45, p55, p57, p65, p71, p80, p99, p101, p127, p133, p135, p145, p157, p173, p177, p179, p189, p203, p205, p207, p209, p211

All the recipes in this book have been created by the editorial team at BBC **olive magazine**.